Mother,

Give Me Your Heart!

MARY JAMES

Editing and Graphic Design by Chris James

ISBN: 978-0-9966267-5-0 (paperback)
ISBN: 978-0-9966267-6-7 (ebook)

To each of my six wonderful children
who gave me the joy of motherhood

Contents

www.ingramcontent.com/pod-product-compliance
Lightning Source LLC
Chambersburg PA
CBHW071849020426
42331CB00007B/1927

* 9 7 8 0 9 9 6 6 2 6 7 5 0 *

About the Author

Mary James has an extraordinary background that gives her credence for providing helpful insights to mothers. Being born near the middle of eight children, she learned to deal with both older and younger siblings—four of whom suffered from severe disabilities. With these critical firsthand learning experiences, Mary witnessed and took an active role in her own mother's challenging child-rearing and homemaking responsibilities.

As a young adult, Mary pursued a degree in education and gained valuable teaching experience (including work with underprivileged children), which further enhanced her great love for children and motherhood.

Later, as a mother of six children of her own, Mary was fully dedicated to caring for them full time. Her devotion to her family created an ideal learning lab for the insights and passion she hopes to share with mothers everywhere.

Mary is also an accomplished musician and piano instructor. She has published her unique piano techniques in the *Learn the Piano* series by James Piano, starting with *Learn the Piano in Five Easy Steps: A Self-Guided Piano Course for Beginners* (available on Amazon and JamesPiano.com).

have in time or all eternity....My prayer is that you will rededicate yourselves to the strengthening of your homes.

—Gordon B. Hinckley, "Walking in the Light of the Lord," *Ensign*, November 1998, 99-100

Dear reader of this book: it is my sincere hope that you will prayerfully incorporate the suggestions and ideas found herein so that your children will reassuringly say (as did the baby bird in this book's introduction), "I *have* a mother! I *know* I do!"...and also say, "she gives me her *heart*!"

Introduction

In the board book for children, "Are You My Mother?" by P.D. Eastman, a baby bird who hatched from an egg while its mother was away searching for food left its nest in search of her. On the baby bird's journey to find its mother, it encountered a kitten, a hen, a dog, then a cow, and longingly asked each, "Are you my mother?" When the animals told the baby bird they were not its mother, the little bird in desperation said, "I have a mother. I know I do. I will find her. I will! I WILL!"

Just then the baby bird saw a "big thing" (a Caterpillar power shovel). "*You* are my mother!" the little bird insisted to the "big thing"...who replied, "SNORT," and proceeded to lift the baby bird up into the air and maneuver it right back into its nest in the tree. "The little bird was home!"...and its mother soon joined it with welcoming food for its first meal.

One can understandably feel the panic of this little bird entering its "new world" without the welcoming *warmth* of its mother to hover over it and calm its fears. But, unlike the mother bird in this story who was the sole provider for her children, many *human* mothers in our world today have the means and support to stay at home and care for their families.

Sadly, however, our homes are likewise becoming motherless institutions. Because of the growing trend to shift a mother's responsibility away from her family—her constant

training, vigilance, companionship and serving as a "watchman" over her children—our homes need to be revitalized in order to keep them intact.

This book delves into the effects of child desertion. It helps mothers know *where* a mother should be and *what* she should be doing. With a Latter-day Saint perspective, it provides practical ideas and helps for all mothers to become better mothers and to focus more on their divine callings. This book is *not* intended to cause mothers to dwell on past mistakes or on unwise past priorities. But rather, its true objective is to motivate mothers to move forward in bringing more *love*, *light* and *sunshine* into their homes.

I do not claim to be an expert in child psychology or counseling, nor do I have any title of child expertise—and I admittedly haven't been a perfect mother. But, being a "stay-at-home" mom of six children and a recipient of a degree in elementary education, I feel I have been blessed with keen insights and unique experiences that help me understand the needs of children and what makes a good mother. With this background, I have a deep yearning to share these insights (and my heart!) with mothers of all stages in hopes that albeit *one* child somewhere may reap their benefits.

—Mary James

Chapter 1

Why Mothers?

I may be the only mother in America who knew where her children were at all times.

—Barbara Bush

Never in the history of the world have women been confronted with so many *decisions*—decisions which fall into two major categories: 1) women *leaving* their homes and families, most often for worldly pursuits, or 2) women *remaining* in their homes to protect and care for their families. Sometimes a woman has no choice but to join the outside workforce, especially if she is single and the sole provider for herself and family. But, too often, the temptations of modern society beckon a woman to needlessly leave her treasured hearth and give up her most important responsibilities to someone else's care.

In another children's book, "Horton Hatches an Egg," by Dr. Seuss, Maisy (a thoughtless mother bird) leaves her nest of unhatched eggs in the care of Horton, a *big-hearted* elephant, to sit on her nest while she flies away to beckoning sandy beaches in a faraway place for fun and relaxation.

Horton is faithful (one hundred percent!) to his trusted assignment and carefully sits and SITS on the small nest of tiny fragile eggs. One day Maisy meanders home to find that her eggs have hatched and—to her dismay—her newborn

babies have grown long, floppy ears and a small elephant trunk! Sadly, because she turned her mothering responsibility over to another, Maisy lost her babies to someone else who more *rightfully* reaped the prized reward.

Mothers, have we also left our coveted "nests?" Have we turned over our children to someone else while we pursue a career or follow a worldly whim for a new home, car, or modern fashions? Or are we entirely focused on our children and their physical, emotional and mental needs? Are we completely involved in their lives? Are our *hearts* and minds centered on them?

Studies have shown that a mother's influence has the most impact on a child. No one else can adequately substitute her nurturing presence in her home. As important as food and shelter are to a child, a mother's love and constant care and direction are just as critical to its total well-being. It doesn't take a "village" to raise a child…or a school or a church or a neighborhood. It takes a *mother!*

Dr. David V. Haws, a medical psychiatrist (and father of the author), affirmed this concern about mother neglect:

> *As important as it is that a mother be available for her children, the number of mothers who have turned to the whims of the 'liberated' woman (which began in the early sixties) is astounding! Mothers at that time who stayed at home to look after their children decreased dramatically, while the rise of working mothers in the decades that followed rose at*

an alarming rate. This is unprecedented and frightening as it has been found that the absence of mothers from their homes greatly endangers their children's emotional and protective well-being.

There should be a move to return the mother to the home. Agitation and unrest in the world today is caused by mothers who left their home and its security for others to reclaim. Because they have abandoned their homes and the proper raising of their families, their children do not have the love and stability they need for developing healthy self images. Without a mother's direction, they can identify with very little in their complex lives.

Just as critical for a mother being *physically* in her home, it is equally important that she be there in *spirit* as well and is cognizant at all times of her children's needs. She should always try to know what they are *thinking* and *feeling*, as well as their *concerns, joys* and *sorrows*—everything about them.

When my children were small and would run into the house from school each day, their first words were invariably, "Mom, where are you?" And when they found me, they would proceed to share their day with me, or tell me what was on their minds—their new friend, their discouragements, their school honors and achievements—and they would show me their backpacks of school papers and awards they had brought home with them.

I have thought many times since those happy "bonding" moments with my children when they would run happily into

the house to seek me out, that if I had allowed myself to be absent from my home during those critical times, I would have missed precious "connecting" moments and a time to encourage and praise them for work well done. I would also have missed out on my greatest *teaching* opportunities as they opened up their hearts and minds to me. This daily interaction with my children also prepared me to direct their homework and home chores, and I knew how to react when I sent them off to school the next morning and prepared them for their day.

At the end of summer as children begin another academic school year, some mothers are heard to exclaim their ecstasy of having their "freedom" back when their children return to school. I never felt that kind of freedom. Since I always enjoyed being with my children, I couldn't identify with such "elation." I felt lost when they were away from me, and I missed them after spending many happy summer hours together.

When a mother is continually absent from her home, her children feel a great "void." Then as mother and child reunite, the child will incessantly cry out for her attention and beg for her love—and for her *heart!*

Maybe this strong love of mother and child began with the developing stages of the child's little embryo tucked securely inside its mother's womb next to her soothing heartbeat. Maybe it was then, that the two hearts of the baby and mother became inseparably connected when the baby entered the world and joined its mother in mortality.

Mothers of all "stages"—let us fight for our coveted place within our families and not turn it thoughtlessly over to others. Let us take back our homes and attach our <u>heartstrings</u> to our children.

Wrap a heartstring of <u>love</u> around your child.

Chapter 2
Mother Case Studies

The act of deserting home in order to shape society is like thoughtlessly removing crucial fingers from an imperiled dike in order to teach people to swim.

—Neal A. Maxwell

There are many examples of critical influences of mothers on their children—influences that are positive, leading to a child's *betterment*, or influences of a negative nature, leading to its *detriment*.

If we were to thoroughly examine our neighborhoods, our schools and some of our homes (even homes of religious backgrounds), we would see firsthand the devastating effects of child *neglect* ("abuse" in many instances), and I think our hearts would burst! We would see teary-eyed children displaying aggressive behavior, desperately vying for their mother's attention, her tender direction, and most importantly her *love*. Silently, also, these same children would plead for the right to have other basic "needs" satisfied—their right to be *happy* and feel *wanted*, *important*, and *appreciated*.

The seven case studies that follow are real-life examples of mothers' influences on their children. For each of these examples, we should focus on the type of influence (negative or positive) of the mother on her child then decide the consequential results of it...how that child was affected.

(It should be noted that most of the negative cases ended in a positive outcome—which, of course, is not the norm, as negative treatment of children often has serious or even *irreversible* consequences.)

Negative Examples of Mother Neglect

Case #1

A few years ago there appeared in a large city newspaper a true story of a boy, then fourteen years old. The story was titled, "The Evolution of a Delinquent." After rehearsing the many serious involvements the boy had had with the law, the reporter posed the question: *"What twisted paths of childhood led to the tortuous road of delinquency?"* Interviews with his neighbors began to supply at least part of the answer.

One neighbor lady said, "I try not to think of [the boy] the way he is now, but how he was when he came to our home and played with our children years ago." Tears filled the woman's eyes as she recalled one afternoon when the young boy, then a small child, rushed to her home after his father had picked him up at a day nursery. As the little boy held on to her hand, she asked, "Why do you always come running to our house when you come home from the nursery?" The little boy replied sorrowfully, *"Because there is no mommy at my house."*

(Note: This woman went on to say that the young boy's answer was heartbreaking, as "there was a mommy at his house and a father also, but many times the children were left at home alone to care for themselves. Often [they] would go

to the neighbors' homes because there was not light or companionship at their own home. They were afraid of the dark. This was not just a darkness that fades with the morning sunlight. You see, there is a darkness that comes when there is no mother there.")

—"Mother, Catch the Vision of your Call," H. Burke Peterson,
April 1974 Conference Report

Case #2

"I was the youngest in a family of nine children—seven girls and two boys. For a reason I never understood, my mother severely mistreated me throughout all my growing up years and would harshly discipline me. I felt *rejected* and *unloved*, and as a consequence, I began stuttering at an early age. This uncontrolled speech impediment was very difficult for me. I was teased incessantly by my classmates and other children and never dated or participated much in social gatherings.

"Growing up without the influence of a loving, caring mother—but feeling that I, myself, was born with the *gift* of Christ and always wanted to 'know Him,' I turned to God and prayer. With His help, I was sustained through a very hard upbringing. Subsequently, throughout my life, I have felt much compassion for others who suffer from difficult situations. I have tried to dedicate my life to helping others."

—Author's name withheld

Case #3

"I was born of parents who loved me greatly in many respects but failed to watch over me at very critical times in my life, especially in my approach to puberty.

"I was baptized into the Church and later ordained a deacon, but I seldom attended church; my father worked on Sundays and my mother did not drive. My mother was a stay-at-home mom, but her heart and interests were often on friends and other things rather than on me and my need for the Church and what was best for me. This was especially true as I neared my teenage years.

"Our family had several camp cots, and it became my custom, along with several neighborhood boys, to sleep outdoors together most summer nights in our yard. Unfortunately, I remember little (if any) supervision from either of my parents during those extended slumber parties, and consequently our 'boy talk' centered on things to which we should not have been exposed.

"Vivid in my memory of this critical time of my youth was the summer of my thirteenth year when my mind was constantly caught up in carnal desires and even intentions to 'experiment' in such vulgar things. Needless to say, at such a young age, I was on the fast track to utter destruction. But somehow…with the *grace* of God, I was spared from carrying out my evil fantasies, unlike some of my other neighborhood friends.

"Summer was soon over...school started, and I was fortunate to find other interests. But, most importantly, just prior to my fourteenth birthday, I was somehow inspired one Sunday to attend an afternoon church meeting, which I did by walking about a mile down a narrow roadway to the church building and sitting among a chapel full of 'strangers' while the Spirit spoke to my heart. My life changed from that moment on. Thereafter, I seldom missed a church meeting and made great progress in my school studies. At the same time, I learned family values from a good friend whose family 'took me in' and gave me a sense of *belonging* while helping me learn correct gospel principles.

"Looking back on my life, I have thought how my parents could have spared me deep *anxieties* and *remorse* during my critical youthful years by watching over me more carefully. I deeply thank Heavenly Father for helping me rise above a very negative and downhill spiral of sin in my life."

—Author's name withheld

Case #4: Life Experiences of a Prison Inmate

"Let me share a few things about my past—not to offer excuses or solicit sympathy, but to show what life-changing experiences can do for a wavering lost soul.

"For virtually all my life, my underlying secret was same-gender attraction or homosexuality. I didn't know what was going on.

"As a young boy, I identified more with Mom than with Dad. But, Mom didn't like me playing with the rough boys

in the neighborhood, so I played with girls. (I desperately wanted to have dolls like they did but wasn't allowed to.) Having lazy eye and not seeing in three dimensions, I could never hit or catch a ball well, and I grew to hate sports. Also, my parents warned me to never fight with other children, so I didn't learn to defend myself from aggression of others. As a consequence of all this—and being a skinny boy and somewhat effeminate, preferring books to sports, refusing to stand up for my rights, and being an only child (for much of my youth) with poor social skills, it isn't any wonder that I made myself a convenient target for bullying and persecution.

"When I was nine years old, my parents adopted my little sister. She had a strong personality and changed our family significantly. She didn't comply easily with my parents' expectations. As a consequence, they generally spanked her a lot—often with Dad using his belt or a paddle. Those were difficult times.

"Since Mom worked at a bakery most days from 4 p.m. to 10 p.m. and Dad didn't get home from his work until 5:30 to 6:00 p.m., it was my job to babysit my sister during their work overlap hours and even some evenings while they attended church meetings or social events. I didn't like babysitting because it encouraged a divisive relationship between my sister and me. I was supposed to 'control' her behavior but not knowing any other form of discipline except my dad's example, I would resort to spanking her. Rightfully, she resented my strong disciplinary action and would tell my parents, which would get me in trouble. That was a 'no-win'

situation, and she and I became adversaries with only an occasional bout of peace and friendship between us.

"Sex was almost a forbidden topic in our home which made me that much more 'curious.' Mom always directed me to Dad with my questions, and Dad was awkward and embarrassed about answering them. So, I soon stopped going to either one of them and instead searched for books in the library where I could find answers. I also misunderstood and learned things I wasn't ready for…and I didn't understand why I didn't get obsessed with girls like other boys. I liked girls, but they didn't 'captivate' me.

"So much changed one day when I was fourteen years old. I was in a gym locker room when a boy, whom I admired, attempted to sexually assault me while a dozen other boys 'looked on,' laughing and taunting me. I never told anyone about this experience, but I think that was when my *double life* started. It was a 'dark and ugly secret' that always ate at me. I learned to compartmentalize it and soon grew numb to it before having periods of promiscuity. What followed years later was…my prison sentence for sexually molesting teenage boys.

"My incarceration resulted in a great blessing for me—even after losing my wife, daughter, church membership, and all my assets. My double life was finally destroyed—'walls of arrogance' were dissolved! My deep dark secret was no longer concealed from those I loved, and I could start over with a clean slate.

"Throughout these many years of prison life, I have been given steady employment and have been able to use my talents and skills in various ways. I have prayed and studied the scriptures daily. I fast every Sunday and attend church services when they are available. I try to daily help and serve my fellow inmates.

"In spite of many harrowing experiences I have had during my incarceration, I have maintained a strong testimony and a fundamental goal to qualify for rebaptism into the Church. I have learned to more fully trust and rely on the Lord as never before. I have witnessed His many tender mercies and have realized that His atonement applies *even* to me. I hope to always follow Him and be a person of worth. My faith is priceless!"

—Author's name withheld

Positive Examples of a Mother's Care

(Cases 5-8; see Chapter 3 for more examples)

Case #5: A Letter From a Son to His Mother

"Mom, I consider myself so blessed to have you as my mother. I have such fond memories of my childhood. You taught us a strong work ethic, organization, responsibility, honesty, frugality, and many more honorable traits. You engendered faith in each of us kids through your example and teachings and through home evening and church attendance. However, at the same time, life was *never* boring…you taught us good humor, planned fun activities and vacations with us,

played practical jokes (which we didn't always appreciate!), and you got us involved in sports and outdoor activities. On top of it all, you served us so well. You helped us strive for excellence in school (even spending late nights typing my school papers), kept a clean and organized home, fed us the most amazing meals on a shoestring budget, baked cookies every Monday, gave us after-school snacks, etc.

"Now that I am an adult, you still continue to make a huge difference in my life. Mom, you are the greatest!"

—Author's name withheld

Case #6

"My exemplar mother's greatest desire was to be a *mother*. Near the temple steps just prior to being married, my father expressed his intention to her of wanting to pursue his educational 'dreams' after their marriage…to which my mother responded that he could study as he wished but *only* if she could match the number of children she aspired to have with his number of degrees. And so began their happy journey together, which included many moves through the years to make it possible for my father to obtain numerous educational goals and my mother to bear eight children.

"I was my mother's third of her eight children. Four of the children were normal as to their health, but one (her last child) died of stomach cancer at the age of four and three others were born with a rare genetic disease that resulted in blindness (appearing around the age of eight) and

degenerative nervous systems, causing grand mal seizures and a loss of limb function. These siblings soon were confined to wheelchairs and eventually became bedridden and died early deaths. (Another brother was diagnosed at the age of two with polio but miraculously recovered.)

"My mother was the main caregiver of her family—which included caring for my father who suffered from Parkinson's disease. Her dedication to her children's complete dependence on her, together with her undying love for them and her strong faith, provided me with the supreme example of devoted motherhood."

—Mary James, author

Case #7

"When my first child was on the way, I had just received my teaching certification and an exciting teaching job offer. Although I had yearned to teach all my life, my priority was my *own* children, and I remained in my home for them—without any regret.

"Being an educator himself, my husband's income was meager, and we could have welcomed an extra monthly paycheck. But, for the sake of our children and my commitment to raising a family, I forsook the temptation that would have given us more material possessions, and I compensated by carefully budgeting. Miraculously, our family did not suffer from such a restricted lifestyle. Our children never thought there could be anything 'better out there,' and

we drew on each other's innovative abilities and talents to make it work. The result was the *togetherness* our family developed and the joy of accomplishment and finding a way to 'make it all happen.'"

—Mary James, author

Case #8: Mother Tributes

"I have attended missionary meetings all over the world and have heard thousands of missionaries tell about their families back home. What do they talk about when they speak of home? They talk about their mothers and the missionaries' deep appreciation for them because of their faithful and devoted training."

—David O. McKay

"My mother was the source from which I derived the guiding principles of my life."

—John Wesley

"All I am I owe to my mother."

—George Washington

"No man is poor who has a loving mother."

—Abraham Lincoln

Wrap a heartstring of devotion around your child.

Chapter 3

Mothering in the Gospel

> *My children are not just my flesh and blood, they are my eternal investment. They, and my righteous husband, are what give me the greatest joy in this life and the greatest hope for life eternal.*
>
> —Mary James

Creating an eternal family should be every parent's most cherished "investment." It is a sacred responsibility Heavenly Father has entrusted in parents to lead His children safely through the perils of this life back home to Him.

We are surrounded today by forces that would destroy home and family. To eradicate these forces, a mother (and father) should always be ready to make a **bold** stand against them and rear their children in righteousness. In accomplishing this, parents need to help their families *believe* and *trust* in Christ.

> *For we labor diligently to persuade our children…to believe in Christ…[W]e talk of Christ, we rejoice in Christ, we preach of Christ…that our children may know to what source they may look for a remission of their sins.*
>
> —2 Nephi 25:23, 26 (emphasis added)

Mothers, the Gospel of Jesus Christ must *radiate* from our lives. We must live the Gospel with conviction and testimony so that our children will respond and also believe. If we exemplify the Savior and make His Spirit felt in the atmosphere of our homes, our children will feel the "warmth" of that Spirit and will develop their own "convictions and testimonies."

A good mother is never complacent in living the Gospel. Her unwavering example helps her children know for themselves what she herself already *knows* and *feels.* Or as Neal A. Maxwell once said, "Parents can only give [their children] what they themselves already have…[their firm beliefs and testimonies]." (Book of Mormon Student Institute Manual, p. 257)

"I am here today," a friend once told me, "because my mother had the courage to act. She lived and taught *correct principles* to her children by acting on *righteous urges.*" (Colleen Bryner)

The Book of Mormon tells of faithful mothers who also acted on *righteous urges* and taught *correct principles* to their children—mothers of the two-thousand stripling warriors who fought with *exactness* and were miraculously preserved in battle because their mothers taught them, "If they did not doubt, God would *deliver* them." Of most significance were the testimonies of these young warriors when they said, "We do not doubt our mothers *knew* it." (Alma 56:47-48, emphasis added)

Moses taught this same axiom to the Israelite parents when he commanded them:

> *Thou shalt love the LORD thy God with all thine heart, and with all they soul, and with all they might. And these words, which I command thee this day, shall be in thine heart:*
>
> *And thou shalt teach them diligently unto thy children, and shalt talk of them when thou sittest in thine house, and when thou walkest by the way, and when thou liest down, and when thou risest up.*
>
> *And thou shalt bind them for a sign upon thine hand, and they shall be as frontlets between thine eyes. And thou shalt write them upon the posts of thy house, and on thy gates.*
>
> —Deuteronomy 6:5-9 (emphasis added)

These verses became a *supreme affirmation* of Jewish prayer and also the custom of placing the written passages into tiny leather boxes to be tied over one's forehead, suggesting that the wearer fulfill this law with "head and heart." In addition, these verses were attached to door frames to "touch or kiss" when entering or leaving a home. (Old Testament Institute Student Manual, p. 218)

Critical gospel living and teaching in the home can best be summarized by Julie B. Beck, a former Relief Society General President of The Church of Jesus Christ of Latter-day Saints, when she said:

The responsibility mothers have today has never required more vigilance. More than at any time in the history of the world, we need mothers who know.... When mothers know who they are and who God is and have made covenants with Him, they will have great power and influence for good on their children.

—"Mothers Who Know," *Ensign*, November 2007, p. 76

Positive Examples of a Mother's Care

(Cases 9-11)

Case #9

"To reinforce the principles that our children were reading and learning in our scripture study, I often used scripture stories as bedtime stories. In later years, my daughter shared how influential this was. She said, 'I think stories that were told over and over again became favorites for us. You sat beside our beds and shared the stories from the scriptures. We loved them and asked to hear them again and again because even at that young age, we could *feel* the spirit of the message they carried and knew the people you were telling us about were valiant and faithful. We wanted to be like them.'

"Children and youth learn best when we help them discover truths for themselves. As they do so, they will feel inspired to love and use the Book of Mormon throughout their lives and will feel equipped to help others do the same."

—Unknown author

Case #10

"My mother taught me the Book of Mormon story and told me that everything depended on whether or not that story was true. I could feel the power of her testimony even as a very small child. And the Spirit bore witness to me that what she told me was true.

"My mother was adept at starting religious discussions with her children. We would all be reading in the front room (education had a high priority in our home), and she would come to the door, maybe with flour on her hands, and say, 'Have you ever wondered about such and such?' And the 'such and such' was always something that generated vigorous discussions about such things as the 'judgment' or 'the degrees of glory' or the events of the 'last days,' (which we understood were about to leap out and grab us any day!). So, most evenings in our home were *family home evenings.*

"One of my mother's favorite questions was this: 'Have you ever thought of the fact that, if Joseph Smith lied about the Book of Mormon, he probably lied about all his revelations—and then we wouldn't have anything?' And she asked it often. I think she wanted that great truth to sink in so deep it would never be forgotten. And it never was. All five of her children were converted.

"I was visited by the Spirit of the Lord and an understanding of the visions of eternity opened up to me. I cannot remember the time when I was not able to 'see' in my mind the progression from intelligence, to pre-mortal spirit, to mortal, to post-mortal spirit, to a resurrected being in the

Celestial Kingdom. I felt that I possessed a grasp of the 'big picture' of Paul and Joseph Smith just as clearly as if I also have been 'caught up to the third heaven' myself. I never doubted the Book of Mormon.

"My mother was the 'missionary' who brought the gospel to me. I have often heard it said that one of the people we love the most is the one who 'brought us the gospel' or, at least, the one who *influenced* us most to accept it. I carry a double portion of love for my mother because she not only went down into the valley of the shadow of death to bring me mortal life...she also managed to penetrate the natural man and bring me the *hope* of eternal life."

—Glenn L. Pearson, "Moroni's Promise, The Converting Power of the Book of Mormon," pgs. 13-16

Case #11: A Mother's Dying Words to Her Children

"I have five minutes to write and tell you what is important. Remember, I love you and want you to be happy. Place your *values* high. Never forfeit these for anything mediocre.

"The gospel is true. Serve others, love all people, and be kind and gentle and honest in every way. Raise your children in truth and righteousness.

"Jesus is the Son of the living God. Remember that He loves you and will guide and direct your footsteps. Stay close to your companions. Work hard and earn your daily bread.

"Serve mankind. Pray always. Remember I love you, as only one who gave you life can love. You are my life and happiness here and into eternity."

—A family friend

Wrap a heartstring of faith around your child.

For Your Child:

WHAT I CAN DO FOR JESUS

- say my prayers
- say something kind
- put my toys away
- help others
- choose the right
- obey my parents
- be sorry when I do something wrong
- don't take what is not mine
- help without being asked
- pay my tithing

- ♥ return things I borrow
- ♥ share with others
- ♥ think what Jesus would have me do
- ♥ give someone a hug
- ♥ be kind to animals
- ♥ say "thank you" and "please"
- ♥ be reverent in church
- ♥ appreciate blessings
- ♥ pray always…at home…and in my heart
- ♥ forgive someone who was unkind to me
- ♥ always be honest
- ♥ always be truthful
- ♥ always be helpful
- ♥ read or listen to scripture stories

—Darren E. Schmidt, "Meaningful Teaching at Home," *Ensign*, January 2013

Chapter 4
A Mother's Palace

Through wisdom is an house builded....[The mother] looketh well to the ways of her household.

—Proverbs 24:3 & 31:27

It has been said that a woman's home is her palace...and so it should be! A woman takes pride in what she does in her palace, and she strives to make it a refuge for her family. It is a place of joy, peace and contentment and where children feel loved and appreciated.

Mothers, in large measure, set the family patterns in her **palace** home. They create the *tone* and *spirit* of the home and establish the *traditions* that have meaning in the lives of their children. Mothers have the most potent influence in determining if the home is a good home and will favorably affect her family.

- A woman's **palace** home is a *clean* home—a clutter-free home. Its physical appearance and orderly arrangement beckons a woman's family to want to be there. The family takes pride in it and wants to be a part of its upkeep. It is their comfort zone when they need refuge from the "world."

- A woman's **palace** home is a *learning* home where children are taught the "lessons of life" and are helped to

be responsible for what happens in it. In this home, they are allowed to do things for themselves and learn family "teamwork" and how to serve each other. They are also taught to be respectful, not only to parents and siblings, but to all others, even those who are different than they are—such as persons with special needs.

- In a "learning" home, a mother directs the *wants* of her children and, together with her husband, distinguishes those things that would be best (of greatest value) for them. In today's world, families may be driven too much by materialism. Mothers can "hold in check" this tendency by cultivating more *simplicity, independence, thrift and economy* in her family. She can set the example of these attributes herself by "patronizing" garage sales and thrift stores or make do (refurbishing) what her family already has.

- In a "learning" home, a mother eliminates habits of *wastefulness* and *idleness* in her family, and she enhances a spirit of *cooperation* from each child to accomplish this. There is a certain satisfaction when family members find ways to cut down unnecessary spending and learn the "art" of sacrifice. (It would also be well if mothers would counteract attitudes in her family of "getting something" without paying the price in personal effort.)

- In a "learning" home, children are taught how to care for their bodies with habits of good *nutrition*,

proper *hygiene*, and personal *grooming.* They also are helped to acquire appetites for healthy foods and encouraged to enjoy regular physical exercise, play and all good habits. In addition, they learn to establish *good character* and feelings of *self worth*.

- Children are also given opportunities to be *independent* in a "learning" home and encouraged to do things on their own—mothers should try not to do things for their children that they can do for themselves. Nor should mothers be bothered when a child is overanxious to verbalize his or her needs, or is too inquisitive about learning something new or just wanting to participate in family talk. (Children are like sponges in their eagerness to learn and experiment—mothers should be patient and careful in answering their questions and satisfying their needs, desires and feelings.)

- Children learn many other things from their mothers in a "learning" home—traits such as attitudes, how to live, how to love (even how to cry!), and children are highly *pliable* and *receptive* to all suggestions, directions, and teachings. Because of this and the intensive learning of the home environment, mothers need to beware that once their children establish habits of thinking and behavior...once beliefs are fixed, it is extremely difficult to modify or change them. Children will most likely carry these traits and/or

behaviors with them throughout their lives. *(Additional learning and teaching techniques are found in Chapter 5.)*

- A woman's **palace** home is a home where *talents* are developed and children's artwork is lovingly displayed on furniture and walls. Children's prized keepsakes should also be treasured and carefully tucked away for safe keeping, and added upon from time to time for journal writing and family history. In this home, mothers praise their children for their artistic abilities and for sharing them with others—she encourages them to enjoy all their good gifts and talents.

- A woman's **palace** home has inviting meals, with children's help in preparing them and a family tradition of eating them together. This home is also a "social center" with movies, talent sharing, backyard games, barbecues, and more. Relatives and friends should always feel welcome and invited to participate in these family activities.

- A woman's **palace** home is also where the family plans and works together for holiday events and celebrations—a place where family *traditions* are made, where meaningful family activities are planned and carried out, and where the family PLAYS together and makes happy memories.

THERE IS POWER IN PLAY

- play creates memories
- play leads to growth
- play creates connection with parents/siblings
- play develops social, communication skills
- play helps with safety and stability
- play softens tensions

Play should be at the top of our priority list. Play every day…be creative with it!

Play in the car ("I spy" games, etc.). Play in the house when doing chores together, such as putting away groceries or folding clothes.

There are two different kinds of play: *deliberate* play (planned play) and *spontaneous* play ('spur-of-the-moment' play such as wrestling, shooting hoops, playing catch, drawing, coloring, etc.).

—Family Rules, "Embrace Family Fun," BYU TV

- A woman's **palace** home is not necessarily a big home—it doesn't have to sit on a hill and be seen, nor does it require modern "face lifts" to look appealing and get attention. It is just a regular home that a family can take pride in and *enjoy.*

- A woman's **palace** home is what the family makes it. Children know it is their "own," and they feel comfortable there.

- A woman's **palace** home is an organized home where parents are in control and where family plans and schedules are made and utilized.

- A woman's **palace** home is where a "queen" lives—a queen who tries to always *be* and *look* her best. In this regal home also resides a "king" whom the queen highly esteems and loves. She encourages her king to bless their children and give them direction, and she supports him with all her heart in his "kingship" responsibilities, as he also supports her in her responsibilities.

- A woman's **palace** home is a Christ-centered home where the Spirit can be felt and heavenly lessons learned. It is a home where kind words are spoken and nothing vile or degrading is allowed within its walls.

In this home, parents reflect the basic spiritual qualities they would teach their family—qualities such as honesty, truthfulness, self-control, loyalty, compassion, kindness, courage, and devotion to the gospel. Here in this sacred

home, parents teach their children to seek after things of *eternal* consequence.

A **palace** home means many other things as well, such as the importance of a mother always being at the *crossroads* of her children—of their coming and going, when they leave and return from school or dates, or when they bring friends home, as Harold B. Lee has counseled:

> *Keep the mother of your home at the "crossroads" of the home. There is a great danger today of homes breaking down because of allurements to entice mothers to neglect their being at home as the family members are coming to or going from the home.*
>
> *Today I feel that women are becoming victims of the speed of modern living. It is in building their motherly intuition and that marvelous closeness with their children that they are enabled to…tune in upon the wavelengths of their children and to pick up the first signs of difficulty, of danger and distress, which if caught in time would save them from disaster.*
>
> "The Righteous Influence of Mothers," Teachings of the Presidents of the Church: Harold B. Lee, Chapter 15

It is absolutely essential that regardless of the children's ages, mothers should always "be there" for them, having total concentration on their *needs*, their *whereabouts*, and *what* they are doing. It is also imperative for mothers to beware that leaving their children unsupervised with another sibling, friend, close relative and sometimes even a "well-intentioned"

babysitter can result in objectionable learning and/or promiscuous activities which can greatly tarnish young lives. (Sleepovers and slumber parties fall into this category, as well, necessitating *strict* parental monitoring.) Mothers should not take any chances on these critical matters.

A **palace** home also requires that a mother be totally concentrated on her household. She must also be able to control the modern devices attacking her home—TV, video games, smartphones, etc. Geoff Steurer, Licensed Marriage and Family Therapist, gives this timely advice for monitoring the use of these devices:

> *If we are to create oneness and connection in our family relationships, we must recognize the splitting of attention that happens when devices infiltrate our family gatherings....[W]e need to put technology in its proper place so that it serves our relationships instead of eroding them.*
>
> *Digital devices are engineered to be irresistible and hard to put down....This dependency on devices is so common that it's easy to ignore how it's affecting us. Young people, therefore, need adults who can model the appropriate use of these devices and can educate children about their effects....[Devices] 'need to be our servants, not our masters.'*

Tips for Managing Digital Devices

- "Delay giving children smartphones and social media accounts until children and teens have developed adequate in-person social skills."

- "Establish family rules and set limits.…Create clear boundaries for when smartphones and devices will be used and then put away.…Invite everyone in the family to be deliberate about taking breaks from their devices on a regular basis…[and] designate a place to put them somewhere out of reach where they can't be accessed easily—in a basket in the kitchen, for example."

- "Avoid mindless gaming and scrolling…[and hold] occasional fasts from games, social media, or other digital distractions." (Referring to the seven-day fast suggested by Russell M. Nelson)

- "Establish digital-free zones [by designating] 'sacred spaces' where devices are never allowed."

—Geoff Steuer, "How to Manage Digital Devices and Get Your Family Back," *Ensign*, February 2020, pp. 30-35

A palace home, then, is a **royal** home. It is a peace-abiding and coveted home that envelops its "subjects" (those who reside there) with Christ-like virtues, contentment, and love. This magnificent "sought-after" home may seem far reaching

to some mothers, but it is my true conviction that most mothers can—with desire, determination, a prayerful heart, and perhaps with small "baby steps"—obtain the "prize" and be rewarded with successful, happy children.

Wrap a heartstring of royalty around your child.

Chapter 5

Teaching in the Home

A mother's heart is a child's schoolroom.

—Henry Ward Beecher

A mother is her child's first teacher—opening the capacities of the child's *body, mind* and *spirit.* Its learning begins when, as a newborn infant, it lies cradled securely in its mother's arms and feels her assured love and bonding influence that will sustain it throughout its life's journey.

The actual teaching process for children begins immediately in the home as parents *talk* to them, *sing* to them, *show* them things, *count* with them, *read* to them...and yes, even teach them to read by pointing to letter names and sounds just as soon as they can form words and learn to talk. Early learning techniques such as these are an important boost to children when we realize that a toddler's personality is already set for life, and its character is formed largely during the first twelve years of his or her life.

All that children learn in their early years is so critical to their overall development and follows them throughout life. "What is placed in the child's brain during the first six years of life is probably there to stay. If you put misinformation into his brain during that period, it is extremely difficult to erase it," explains Dr. Glenn Doman (a prominent author

and renowned scientist) about his lifetime research on child development.

It may seem common philosophy to leave all of the teaching of our children to schools. But I would contend that no school can make up for gaps caused by parents' failure to teach their children in the home—schools only *enhance* the learning background parents give their children. Therefore, it is erroneous for parents to think that the job of teaching their children is finished once their children begin school, when in fact, it has only begun and should continue to be parents' priority throughout their children's growing years.

There are many ways a mother can teach her children good learning skills in their early years. She begins by helping them "chart" the course of their lives by encouraging them to learn *independence* and doing things for themselves—also helping them develop *self confidence* and find creative ways to solve problems and make their own decisions.

A mother should teach her children good work habits and help them experience the satisfaction of *accomplishment* and a job well done. She should let them share in family work projects such as gardening and yard care and assign them regular house chores such as keeping their beds made and rooms clean (a daily work chart will help accomplish this) and encourage them to help younger siblings with their chores as well. A good mother works (and plays) alongside her children in all their tasks and enjoyments. She also helps her children discover that the world does not "revolve" around them and that they are happier when they focus on improving themselves and their environment.

Teaching Idea

Teach your child how to do a particular job and put him/her in charge of it for a week.

—Darren E. Schmidt, "Meaningful Teaching at Home," *Ensign*, January 2013

As stated earlier, a good mother teaches her children to read, and she starts them along this path when they are young. She also helps them develop a love for reading by visiting the library often with them and being a good role model of reading herself. She can make reading fun and sometimes social by having them read to another family member, a pet, a stuffed animal, a doll, etc. She could also provide a special "book corner" or a favorite reading spot in her home where her children will gravitate to often…as reminisced by Gordon B. Hinckley about his childhood home:

> *When I was a boy, we lived in a large old house. One room was called the library. It had a solid table and a good lamp, three or four comfortable chairs with good light and books in cases that lined the walls. There were many volumes—the acquisitions of my father and mother over a period of many years.*

We were never forced to read them, but they were placed where they were handy and where we could get at them whenever we wished. There was quiet in that room. It was understood that it was a place to study.

There were also magazines in this room—the Church magazines and two or three other good magazines. There were books of history and literature, books on technical subjects, dictionaries, a set of encyclopedias, and an atlas of the world. It was an environment of learning. In so many of our homes today there is not the possibility of such a library. Most families are crammed for space. But with planning there can be a corner…an area that becomes something of a hideaway from the noises about us where one can sit and read and think.

Begin early in exposing children to books. The mother who fails to read to her small children does a disservice to them and a disservice to herself. It takes time, yes, much of it. It takes self-discipline. It takes organizing and budgeting the minutes and hours of the day. But it will never be a bore as you watch young minds come to know characters, expressions, and ideas. Good reading can become a love affair, far more fruitful in long term effects than many other activities in which children use their time.

—Gordon B. Hinckley, "Some Lessons I Learned As a Boy," *Ensign*, May 1993

In addition to teaching the *love* of reading, a mother can encourage her children to memorize favorite stories, nursery

rhymes, poems, etc. She could also provide them with maps of places and help them learn about historical events that would enhance their appreciation of the world around them.

Mothers should teach their children that their family is eternal and that each family member must work together for unity and love in their home. A mother should also encourage cooperation within her family and help her children find ways to serve each other so that peace and harmony can prevail in the home.

Teaching Idea

Give each child clear communication about a family unity rule you want emphasized more in your home. After a week of practicing the rule, let children discuss how they accomplished the rule and how it benefited the family. Consistently follow through with the same rule until it becomes commonplace.

There are many other teaching techniques that good mothers can use with their children. Depending on the children's ages, these techniques could include:

- ♥ Teaching them numbers, alphabet, colors, patterns, shapes, and how to tell time.
- ♥ Providing them with learning games, problem solving (such as doubling a recipe), contests (coloring and drawing, spelling bees), puzzles, and road trips.
- ♥ Promoting good literature and music in the home and the best in art entertainment.
- ♥ Making opportunities for them to learn *new* things in everyday activities.
- ♥ Reinforcing their learning by "picking their brains"—also following up with their school assignments and encouraging them to set high goals in their grades.
- ♥ Concentrating on their *good* points, not their failures—always finding opportunities to praise them.
- ♥ Helping them make choices, learn to solve problems and follow instructions for multiple tasks or steps.
- ♥ Teaching them *self-reliance* and the importance of preparing for the future.
- ♥ Building their *confidence* and feelings of self worth and letting them know that their ideas are important and appreciated.

- Letting their learning be a *personal* and satisfying accomplishment—not to brag about or show off.

- Making learning *fun* and showing excitement for what they learn. (Mothers should be sensitive to the moods and interests of her children and not "overdo" their learning as they may rebel if pushed too much.)

- Not fostering *competition* between siblings—"competitiveness" can produce lifetime rivalry in families.

- Trying to get the best teaching results from the first child so that younger siblings can be provided with a good example...and parents' teaching job made easier!

In addition to the above teaching techniques, it is critical that mothers verbalize clear instructions to their children about rules for conduct in their homes and what will happen if those rules are not obeyed. Consistent follow-through with consequences for children's failure to obey rules should be a parent's priority in teaching them to be responsible for learning good behavior. (Children should know that choices have *consequences*—that they simply cannot *do* whatever they want and then have things work out exactly *how* they want it.)

With all this said, probably the singular most important aspect in teaching children and promoting an atmosphere of learning in the home is for parents to maintain proper discipline (home management) with their children. Good parental discipline teaches children *obedience* and *self-control*

so they will want to listen and follow family rules and directions.

The word "discipline" is often equated with punishment or harshness rather than the meanings of *love*, *respect*, *learner*, or "*follower of Christ*" associated with "disciple"—derived from the same Latin root word. If we readily apply the "disciple" definition in managing our homes, our children will be more apt to respond to it…but <u>only</u> if we combine it with some *firmness* (resoluteness!) will it be effective.

Surprisingly, good discipline begins with an infant. When a mother establishes her baby's feeding, sleeping, and playing schedules and is *consistent* in enforcing them, she is maintaining control—not her baby. It is also important for mothers to recognize her baby's legitimate crying needs so she can adequately give "deserving" attention to it—she should never be overanxious to pacify each cry without first assessing the reason. (A mother's *firm* management of her baby's beginning habits and schedules is not a selfish motive—it is for the baby's independence and well-being as well as for her own need of rest and personal space.)

As a child grows, consistent discipline continues to be required in order to differentiate between needs and wants. A mother should be ever cognizant of her child's *needs* but not always his or her *wants*—as "wants" can be a baby's controlling mechanism. Children can most often learn to satisfy their own wants and, if encouraged to do so, will develop the self control and *independence* that will help sustain them throughout their lives.

Along with consistency in establishing guidelines for children, mothers should strive to establish *positive* ways to correct and discipline their children. This is accomplished through deep love, firm direction, and clear expectations for each child—she should never expect her children to have to "guess" what she wants or expects of them. She must always say what she *means* and *mean* what she says.

Example of *Positive* Disciplinary Action

Instead of directing her young child with words such as, "Don't touch that!" a mother can find an object to *replace* the "untouchable" one then calmly say, "You can play with this instead…it is softer, prettier, and more fun," and gently draw the child's attention to the "better" choice. With this approach, the child will inevitably switch over to the new "command" without tears or a tantrum. Children are quick to respond to these types of "changes" if they are handled in a *positive*, loving way.

Example of *Firm* Direction

When a mother gives clear instructions to her child such as: *"It's time to get ready for bed,"* or *"You need to put away your toys,"* her command should be obeyed by the child without a firm repetition of, "I *told* you it is time for bed," or "Put away your toys *now*!"

Depending on the circumstances and the child's attitude, a *positive* warning may first be given to prevent a child's resistance to a command such as, "You can play for ten more minutes then…off to bed!" This extended privilege should

then be strictly adhered to or the child should lose future privileges.

Positive disciplinary approaches may at times need to be replaced with firmer commands, such as when a child raises his or her voice or *defiantly* breaks rules or *refuses* to listen to directions. In this case, a parent should reiterate with firmness the *inappropriate* behavior of the child then take the necessary steps to help the child amend its ways. If his or her behavior continues to be unacceptable, a "timeout corner" or "solitary confinement" in the child's room, or a "make-up chore" might be necessary until the appropriate consequences are met. Parents should <u>never</u> dismiss a child's "defiant" behavior without asserting meaningful consequences.

A "last resort" disciplinary action, such as spanking, might be considered when a child persists in resisting a parent's more patient approach. A rebellious child may need to experience some physical pain to change unacceptable behavior or feel remorse after causing pain to someone else. This "ultimate" disciplinary action should be used *sparingly*, not with harshness or anger, and finished with an increase of love. If spanking becomes a regular occurrence, it then is inappropriate and meaningless to the child and may encourage more defiant behavior.

It is my belief that children who are rebellious must at times experience some painful consequences for unacceptable behavior while they are young in order to escape greater "unavoidable" pain later in their lives. Even Heavenly Father uses "physical" punishment and "painful" justice for wickedness and unrepented sin. He also does not force any of

His children to correct their ways but helps them know that obedience is for their *good*, their *learning*, and for His *blessings*. He never gives up on us for misbehavior—neither should we ever give up on our children for the same reason.

At the end of this critical chapter on how we can better teach and correct our children, we should keep in mind that children are happiest when they are *busy*...when they are *learning*...and when they are *disciplined.*

Wrap a heartstring of positive teaching around your child.

- *Today*...compliment each child on something you like about him or her that you haven't mentioned for awhile.

- *Today*...take an evening walk with your family and talk about our beautiful world and the love Heavenly Father has for His children to make it for them.

- *Today*...surprise each child with a little gift: candy bar, book, etc.

- *Today*...place "I think you are special because..." notes and put them in each child's lunch, pocket, shoe, etc.

- *Today*...start a "favorite dessert" week by making each child's favorite dessert one day of the week.

- *Today*...work on being more patient or overcoming a weakness that keeps you from feeling closer to your children.

- *Today*...recall the "miracle of birth" you felt for each of your children.

- *Today*...give extra hugs to your children.

- *Today*...make your home an extra clean and i[illegible] place for your family.
- *Today*...do something you have procrastinated doing for your family: favorite meal, family photo day, etc.
- *Today*...give each child his own special time with you *alone* (15 minutes). Talk about special needs, problems, aspirations, etc.
- *Today*...do a special craft with your children.
- *Today*...try to keep calm under all circumstances.
- *Today*...read a bedtime story with all your children together on your bed. Snuggle up and have fun!
- *Today*...use loving and positive approaches with your children.
- *Today*...play an outdoor sport with your family.
- *Today*...place personal notes under the pillows of your children, expressing your love and appreciation for each of them.
- *Today*...emphasize the good qualities of each child.
- *Today*...fix a favorite after-school snack for your children and set it in a "special place."
- *Today*...refrain from being negative in dealing with your children—speak, act and discipline in a positive way.

- *Today*…make your thoughts and actions those that you would want your children to emulate.
- *Today*…smile a lot!
- *Today*…do not raise your voice.
- *Today*…make your children feel important, complimenting them on what they do well.
- *Today*…play a game with your children.
- *Today*…write an "I'm proud of you because…" note and send in it in the mail to each of your children (on separate days of the week).
- *Today*…do more listening and less talking.
- *Today*…have a sense of humor with your children. Help them see that life need not always be serious.
- *Today*…paste “I love my family!” notes around your home.
- *Today*…begin a daily habit of praying more frequently for better family relationships (more congeniality…peace, love, etc.).

Give your child a bouquet of heartstrings and save a precious life.

Love, Devotion, Faith, Royalty, and Positive Teaching

“Ultimate” Case Study

Mother of a Prophet

The Restoration of the Gospel Was a “Family Affair.”

“The Lord had watched over Joseph Smith’s ancestors for generations. He had His eye on them from the beginning of time up to 1820 when He and His Beloved Son visited Joseph and began the preparation for him to become the Prophet of the Restoration of the fullness of the gospel in this last dispensation.

It was decreed in the councils of eternity, long before the foundations of the earth were laid, that he should be the man, in the last dispensation of this world, to bring forth the word of God to the people, and receive the fulness of the keys and power of the

Priesthood of the Son of God. The Lord had his eye upon him, and upon his father, and upon his father's father, and upon their progenitors clear back to Abraham, and from Abraham to the flood, from the flood to Enoch, and from Enoch to Adam. He has watched that family and that blood as it has circulated from its fountain to the birth of that man.

—Brigham Young, Journal of Discourses, Vol. 7, p. 289 (emphasis added)

"Joseph Smith thus brought with him generations of good, stalwart, God-fearing people—progenitors who sought diligently for religion and a good life. Many of them paid a great price to establish the *freedom of religion* essential for him to come to earth to fulfill his mission. There were hundreds, perhaps even thousands, who were protesters of Christendom during the dark ages of the Great Apostasy, many of whom gave their lives for the right of all people to worship God according to the dictates of their own conscience. Some of these protesters were John Wycliffe, Martin Luther, and William Tyndale.

"The hand of the Lord became even more evident in the life of a special reformer, John Lathrop, who was born in 1584 in Yorkshire, England. A minister in the Church of England, John Lathrop declared that the gospel should be taught more freely to the common people and that they should be able to read the Bible for themselves. He was arrested for his teachings and released on the condition he would leave England. He came to America with his children and followers—the Mack family were *descendants* of John

Lathrop. He was the fourth-great-grandfather of Lucy Mack Smith.

"In 1638 another man, Robert Smith, emigrated from England to the new world. His posterity included Samuel Smith, a captain in George Washington's army, and Asael Smith, who fought in the Revolutionary War. Asael Smith's son was Joseph Smith Sr., who married Lucy Mack Smith. They are the *parents* of the Prophet Joseph Smith Jr.

"We can see the *believing blood* that flowed in the veins of the Smith family. The hand of God was working from the very beginning to prepare for the Restoration of the gospel through this tapestry of faith woven through the generations of time. The result is the true Church of Jesus Christ spreading throughout the earth."

—M. Russell Ballard, "Tapestry of God's Hand," Church News, February 19, 2011 (emphasis added)

Living the Gospel and Being Exalted was Also a "Family Affair."

Joseph Sr. and Lucy Mack Smith were the parents of eleven children, seven boys and four daughters. Joseph and Lucy taught their children religious precepts and encouraged the study of the Bible and to have faith and love of God. Never was there a more obedient family.

Joseph Smith Jr. grew up on the family farm and was almost exclusively under his family's influence. During his formative years, he began to incorporate and manifest

qualities that would help him fulfill his foreordained mission…he developed strong *family bonds* and learned to *work hard, think for himself, serve others,* and *love liberty.*

Joseph Smith Sr. — Father of the Prophet

Joseph Smith Sr. was first a "seeker." He believed the Bible but not the theologies of his day. He also believed in his son's visions, and he physically protected him during the translation of the plates. His total loyalty to the Restored Church is itself a strong argument for the *authenticity* of the prophetic mission of his son.

Joseph Sr. often had prophetic visions and dreams and strong *intimations* of the coming forth of the Restoration of the Gospel.

Lucy Mack Smith — Mother of the Prophet

Lucy was a mother of unrelented religious beliefs. Her exemplary faith helped her children endure life's challenges and be steadfast to the restored gospel truths. She also nurtured the budding faith of each of her children by teaching them to read and love the Bible and to pray and honor God.

Lucy warned other parents to be accountable for their children's conduct and advised them to "give their children books to read and teach them how to *work* to keep them from idleness." She also encouraged parents to teach their children to be "full of love, goodness and kindness, and never do in secret what they would not do in the presence of millions."

When young Joseph, at fourteen years of age, related to his mother the glorious appearance of God the Father and his Son, Jesus Christ, she believed with *all her heart.* Her soul rejoiced in the gradual day-to-day unfolding of the restoration of the true gospel for which she had so long awaited. She was justifiably proud of the mission and achievements of her son and family.

A woman of great *empathy* and *compassion*, Lucy displayed prayerful concern over the Prophet and her family long before they were hunted and persecuted. She seemed intuitively to know when her children needed her prayers most. She led the whole family in prayer each day for young Joseph to be instructed in his duty and protected from the snares of Satan.

Lucy was also *patient, encouraging*, and *perceptive* while Joseph was suffering through four long years of "tested growth" until Moroni finally entrusted the plates and that part of the work of the restoration to him. She loved the Book of Mormon and bore a powerful testimony of its truths to all who would listen.

The Lord had prepared Lucy for her critical role as the *mother* of a Latter-day Saint prophet through her own intelligent and devoted mother, Lydia Gates Mack. Lydia had been a schoolteacher from a wealthy and cultured family before her marriage to Solomon Mack. Her teaching background was a great blessing to their family. Because of Solomon's frequent work absences from the home, the responsibility for their children's *temporal, intellectual, and spiritual* welfare devolved upon her. She not only taught them school subjects, but also called them together both morning

and evening to pray. Additionally, they were taught to *love* each other and to *love* and honor God.

Lucy inherited her mother's *self-reliance*, *refinement*, and great exceptional *gift* of language. Lucy wrote valuable diaries, letters, and biographies in a day of frontier life when there was little time for writing. Lucy passed her language skills on to her Prophet son who also became gifted in speaking and writing—all of which helped him in charting the course of the restored gospel.

Lucy's appreciation and love for her mother is reflected in poignant words of parting from her when Lucy and her family moved from Vermont to Palmyra, New York. Of that sad departure, Lucy wrote that she had *"to take leave of that pious and affectionate parent to whom I am indebted for all the religious instructions as well as most of the educational privileges which I have ever received."*

Lucy considered motherhood her most cherished responsibility. Her "treasure" was her family, and she merited the prophetic tribute that her beloved husband gave to her on his deathbed: *"Mother, do you not know, that you are the mother of as great a family as ever lived upon the earth?"* Joseph also paid tribute to his mother when, during the dark days of persecution in 1842, he wrote: "*My mother is one of the noblest and best of all women.*"

—Source: Lucy Mack Smith, "The History of Joseph Smith by His Mother," 1853

Final Thoughts

America is slipping from its moral foundations. This great crisis has been caused and will continue to increase because of failure in the home.

—Pastor John Hagee, "Life, Liberty and Levin," Fox News, December 2019 (emphasis added)

America is slipping! Its values are eroding and children are being "shortchanged" as mothers leave their homes and families—most often not out of necessity, but for worldly pleasure, self-gratification and larger salaries.

The light in many of our homes has gone out. Beckoning rays of sunshine have been replaced by daycare centers, babysitters and 'electronic' sitters [devices].

—Simon Collins, "Put Family Before Moneymaking Is Message from Festival," New Zealand Herald, Feb. 1, 2010

Mothers! We need to bring "light" and "sunshine" back into our homes and remember it is not about "us" but of loving, caring and protecting our children…and making *eternal* families.

[Mothers], guard your children….Nothing is more precious to you as mothers, absolutely nothing. Your children are the most valuable thing you will